Table of Contents

List of Appendices

Appendix A: NEPAnet and How to Use It

Appendix B: The Federal Register and How to Use It

Appendix C: EPA's EIS Rating System

Appendix D: Agency NEPA Contacts

Appendix E: Some Useful Definitions from the Council on
Environmental Quality NEPA Implementing
Regulations

List of Acronyms

CE:	Categorical Exclusion
CEQ:	Council on Environmental Quality
CFR:	Code of Federal Regulations
EA:	Environmental Assessment
EIS:	Environmental Impact Statement
EMS:	Environmental Management System
EPA:	The Environmental Protection Agency
FONSI:	Finding of No Significant Impact
NEPA:	The National Environmental Policy Act
NOI:	Notice of Intent
ROD:	Record of Decision

Purpose of the Guide

This guide has been developed to help citizens and organizations who are concerned about the environmental effects of federal decisionmaking to effectively participate in Federal agencies' environmental reviews under the National Environmental Policy Act (NEPA).[1] With some limited exceptions, all Federal agencies in the executive branch have to comply with NEPA before they make final decisions about federal actions that could have environmental effects. Thus, NEPA applies to a very wide range of federal actions that include, but are not limited to, federal construction projects, plans to manage and develop federally owned lands, and federal approvals of non-federal activities such as grants, licenses, and permits. The Federal Government takes hundreds of actions every day that are, in some way, covered by NEPA.

The environmental review process under NEPA provides an opportunity for you to be involved in the Federal agency decisionmaking process. It will help you understand what the Federal agency is proposing, to offer your thoughts on alternative ways for the agency to accomplish what it is proposing, and to offer your comments on the agency's analysis of the environmental effects of the proposed action and possible mitigation of potential harmful effects of such actions. NEPA requires Federal agencies to consider environmental effects that include, among others, impacts on social, cultural, and economic resources, as well as natural resources. Citizens often have valuable information about places and resources that they value and the potential environmental, social, and economic effects that proposed federal actions may have on those places and resources. NEPA's requirements provide you the means to work with the agencies so they can take your information into account.

---

[1] National Environmental Policy Act of 1969, *as amended,* 42 U.S.C. §§ 4321-4347, available at *www.nepa.gov.*

History and Purpose of NEPA

Congress enacted NEPA in December, 1969, and President Nixon signed it into law on January 1, 1970. NEPA was the first major environmental law in the United States and is often called the "Magna Carta" of environmental laws. Importantly, NEPA established this country's national environmental policies.

To implement these policies, NEPA requires agencies to undertake an assessment of the environmental effects of their proposed actions prior to making decisions. Two major purposes of the environmental review process are better informed decisions and citizen involvement, both of which should lead to implementation of NEPA's policies.

Who is Responsible for Implementing NEPA?

Every agency in the executive branch of the Federal Government has a responsibility to implement NEPA. In NEPA, Congress directed that, to the fullest extent possible, the policies, regulations, and public laws of the United States shall be interpreted and administered in accordance with the policies set forth in NEPA.[2] To implement NEPA's policies, Congress prescribed a procedure, commonly referred to as "the NEPA process" or "the environmental impact assessment process."

NEPA's procedural requirements apply to all Federal agencies in the executive branch. NEPA does not apply to the President, to Congress, or to the Federal courts.[3]

Because NEPA implementation is an important responsibility of the Federal Government, many Federal agencies have established offices dedicated to NEPA policy and program oversight. Employees in these offices prepare NEPA guidance, policy, and procedures for the agency, and often make this information available to the public through sources such as Internet websites. Agencies are required to develop their own capacity within a NEPA program in order to develop analyses and documents (or review those prepared by others) to ensure informed decisionmaking.[4] Most agency NEPA procedures are available on-line at the NEPAnet website *http://ceq.eh.doe.gov/nepa/ regs/agency/agencies.cfm*). Agency NEPA procedures are published in

---

[2] Section 102 of the National Environmental Policy Act of 1969, 42 U.S.C. §4332.

[3] CEQ NEPA Regulations 40 C.F.R.§1508.12.

[4] Council on Environmental Quality , "Regulations for Implementing the Procedural Provisions of the National Environmental Policy Act" 40 C.F.R. section 1507.2, available at *www.nepa.gov*. Future references to the CEQ NEPA Regualtions will be cited as : CEQ NEPA Regulations, 40 C.F.R. §1507.2.

National Environmental Policy Act Sec. 101
[42 USC § 4331]

(a) The Congress, recognizing the profound impact of man's activity on the interrelations of all components of the natural environment, particularly the profound influences of population growth, high-density urbanization, industrial expansion, resource exploitation, and new and expanding technological advances and recognizing further the critical importance of restoring and maintaining environmental quality to the overall welfare and development of man, declares that it is the continuing policy of the Federal Government, in cooperation with State and local governments, and other concerned public and private organizations, to use all practicable means and measures, including financial and technical assistance, in a manner calculated to foster and promote the general welfare, to create and maintain conditions under which man and nature can exist in productive harmony, and fulfill the social, economic, and other requirements of present and future generations of Americans.

(b) In order to carry out the policy set forth in this Act, it is the continuing responsibility of the Federal Government to use all practicable means, consistent with other essential considerations of national policy, to improve and coordinate Federal plans, functions, programs, and resources to the end that the Nation may —

1. fulfill the responsibilities of each generation as trustee of the environment for succeeding generations;

2. assure for all Americans safe, healthful, productive, and aesthetically and culturally pleasing surroundings;

3. attain the widest range of beneficial uses of the environment without degradation, risk to health or safety, or other undesirable and unintended consequences;

4. preserve important historic, cultural, and natural aspects of our national heritage, and maintain, wherever possible, an environment which supports diversity, and variety of individual choice;

5. achieve a balance between population and resource use which will permit high standards of living and a wide sharing of life's amenities; and

6. enhance the quality of renewable resources and approach the maximum attainable recycling of depletable resources.

(c) The Congress recognizes that each person should enjoy a healthful environment and that each person has a responsibility to contribute to the preservation and enhancement of the environment.

the Federal Register for public review and comment when first proposed and some are later codified and published in the Code of Federal Regulations.[5] If you experience difficulty locating an agency's NEPA procedures, you can write or call the agency NEPA point of contacts and ask for a copy of their procedures.[6]

To What Do the Procedural Requirements of NEPA Apply?

In NEPA, Congress recognized that the Federal Government's actions may cause significant environmental effects. The range of actions that cause significant environmental effects is broad and includes issuing regulations, providing permits for private actions, funding private actions, making federal land management decisions, constructing publicly-owned facilities, and many other types of actions. Using the NEPA process, agencies are required to determine if their proposed actions have significant environmental effects and to consider the environmental and related social and economic effects of their proposed actions.

NEPA's procedural requirements apply to a Federal agency's decisions for actions, including financing, assisting, conducting, or approving projects or programs; agency rules, regulations, plans, policies, or procedures; and legislative proposals.[7] NEPA applies when a Federal agency has discretion to choose among one or more alternative means of accomplishing a particular goal.[8]

Frequently, private individuals or companies will become involved in the NEPA process when they need a permit issued by a Federal agency. When a company applies for a permit (for example, for crossing federal lands or impacting waters of the United States) the agency that is being asked to issue the permit must evaluate the environmental effects of the permit decision under NEPA. Federal agencies might require the private company or developer to pay for the preparation of analyses, but the agency remains responsible for the scope and accuracy of the analysis.

---

[5] The draft agency implementing procedures, or regulations, are published in the Federal Register, and a public comment period is required prior to CEQ approval. Commenting on these agency regulations is one way to be involved in their development. Most agencies already have implementing procedures; however, when they are changed, the agency will again provide for public comment on the proposed changes.

[6] See Appendices A and D for information on how to access agency points of contact and agency websites.

[7] CEQ NEPA Regulations, 40 C.F.R. § 1508.18. Note that this section applies only to legislation drafted and submitted to Congress by federal agencies. NEPA does not apply to legislation initiated by members of Congress.

[8] CEQ NEPA Regulations, 40 C.F.R. § 1508.23.

When Does NEPA Apply?

NEPA requires agency decisionmakers to make informed decisions. Therefore, the NEPA process must be completed before an agency makes a final decision on a proposed action. Good NEPA analyses should include a consideration of how NEPA's policy goals (Section 101) will be incorporated into the decision to the extent consistent with other considerations of national policy. NEPA does not require the decisionmaker to select the environmentally preferable alternative or prohibit adverse environmental effects. Indeed, decisionmakers in Federal agencies often have other concerns and policy considerations to take into account in the decisionmaking process, such as social, economic, technical or national security interests. But NEPA does require that decisionmakers be informed of the environmental consequences of their decisions.

The NEPA process can also serve to meet other environmental review requirements. For instance, actions that require the NEPA process may have an impact on endangered species, historic properties, or low income communities. The NEPA analysis, which takes into account the potential impacts of the proposed action and investigates alternative actions, may also serve as a framework to meet other environmental review requirements, such as the Endangered Species Act, the National Historic Preservation Act, the Environmental Justice Executive Order, and other Federal, State, Tribal, and local laws and regulations.[9]

Who Oversees the NEPA Process?

There are three Federal agencies that have particular responsibilities for NEPA. Primary responsibility is vested in the Council on Environmental Quality (CEQ), established by Congress in NEPA. Congress placed CEQ in the Executive Office of the President and gave it many responsibilities, including the responsibility to ensure that Federal agencies meet their obligations under the Act. CEQ oversees implementation of NEPA, principally through issuance and interpretation of NEPA regulations that implement the procedural requirements of NEPA. CEQ also reviews and approves Federal agency NEPA procedures, approves of alternative arrangements for compliance with NEPA in the case of emergencies, and helps to resolve disputes between Federal agencies and with other governmental entities and members of the public.

---

[9] CEQ NEPA Regualtions, 40 C.F.R. § 1502.25.

In 1978, CEQ issued binding regulations directing agencies on the fundamental requirements necessary to fulfill their NEPA obligations.[10] The CEQ regulations set forth minimum requirements for agencies. The CEQ regulations also called for agencies to create their own implementing procedures that supplement the minimum requirements based on each agency's specific mandates, obligations, and missions.[11] These agency-specific NEPA procedures account for the slight differences in agencies' NEPA processes.

The Environmental Protection Agency's (EPA) Office of Federal Activities reviews environmental impact statements (EIS) and some environmental assessments (EA) issued by Federal agencies.[12] It provides its comments to the public by publishing summaries of them in the Federal Register, a daily publication that provides notice of Federal agency actions.[13] EPA's reviews are intended to assist Federal agencies in improving their NEPA analyses and decisions.[14]

Another government entity involved in NEPA is the U.S. Institute for Environmental Conflict Resolution, which was established by the Environmental Policy and Conflict Resolution Act of 1998 to assist in resolving conflict over environmental issues that involve Federal agencies.[15] While part of the Federal Government (it is located within the Morris K. Udall Foundation, a Federal agency located in Tucson, Arizona), it provides an independent, neutral, place for Federal agencies to work with citizens as well as State, local, and Tribal governments, private organizations, and businesses to reach common ground. The Institute provides dispute resolution alternatives to litigation and other adversarial approaches. The Institute is also charged with assisting the Federal Government in the implementation of the substantive policies set forth in Section 101 of NEPA.[16]

---

[10] CEQ NEPA Regulations, 40 C.F.R. parts 1500-1508, available at *www.nepa.gov.*

[11] CEQ NEPA Regualations, 40 C.F.R. § 1507.3.

[12] Clean Air Act, 42 U.S.C. § 7609.

[13] See Appendix B for information on the Federal Register.

[14] For additional infomation see *http://www.epa.gov/compliance/nepa/index.htm.*

[15] Environmental Policy and Conflict Resolution Act of 1998, 20 U.S.C. §§ 5601-5609.

[16] For a discussion of the relationship between Section 101 of NEPA and conflict resolution, including specific case examples and recommendations for strengthening that relationship see the National Environmental Conflict Resolution Advisory Committee, "Final Report — Submitted to the U.S. Institute for Environmental Conflict Resolution of the Morris K. Udall Foundation," (April 2005), available at *http://www.ecr.gov* by clicking on "Resources" and "NEPA and ECR.".

Navigating the NEPA Process

Each year, thousands of Environmental Assessments (EAs) and hundreds of Environmental Impact Statements (EISs) are prepared by Federal agencies. These documents provide citizens and communities an opportunity to learn about and be involved in each of those environmental impact assessments that are part of the Federal agency decisionmaking process. It is important to understand that commenting on a proposal is not a "vote" on whether the proposed action should take place. Nonetheless, the information you provide during the EA and EIS process can influence the decisionmakers and their final decisions because NEPA does require that federal decisionmakers be informed of the environmental consequences of their decisions.

This guide will help you better navigate through the NEPA process and better understand the roles of the various other actors. While reading the guide, please refer to the following flowchart, "The NEPA Process," which details the steps of the NEPA process. For ease of reference, each step of the process is designated with a number which is highlighted in the text discussing that particular step. While agencies may differ slightly in how they comply with NEPA, understanding the basics will give you the information you need to work effectively with any agency's process.

The NEPA Process

```
┌─────────────────────────────────────┐
│ 1. Agency Identifies a Need for Action │
│       and Develops a Proposal          │
└─────────────────────────────────────┘
                 │
                 ▼
┌─────────────────────────────────────┐
│   2. Are Environmental Effects Likely  │
│          to Be Significant?            │
└─────────────────────────────────────┘
```

NO ——————————————— YES

3. Proposed Action is Described in Agency Categorical Exclusion (CE)

— NO →

5. Significant Environmental Effects Uncertain or No Agency CE

8. Significant Environmental Effects May or Will Occur

YES ↓

YES →

6. Develop Environmental Assessment (EA) with Public Involvement to the Extent Practicable

9. Notice of intent to prepare Environmental Impact Statement (EIS)

↓

10. Public Scoping and Appropraite Public Involvement

4. Does the Proposal Have Extraordinary Circumstances?

YES →

Significant Environmental Effects?

11. Draft EIS

NO ↓

12. Public Review and Comment and Appropriate Public Involvement

NO ↓

7. Finding of No Significant Impact

13. Final EIS

14. Public Availability of FEIS

Decision

15. Record of Decision

Implementation with Monitoring as Provided in the Decision

Significant new circumstances or information relevant to environmental concerns or substantial changes in the proposed action that are relevant to environmental concerns may necessitate preparation of a supplemental EIS following either the draft or final EIS or the Record of Decision (CEQ NEPA Regulations, 40 C.F.R. § 1502.9(c)).

The NEPA process begins when an agency develops a proposal to address a need to take an action.

The need to take an action may be something the agency identifies itself, or it may be a need to make a decision on a proposal brought to it by someone outside of the agency, for example, an applicant for a permit. Based on the need, the agency develops a proposal for action (Number 1 in Figure 1). If it is the only Federal agency involved, that agency will automatically be the "lead agency," which means it has the primary responsibility for compliance with NEPA.

Some large or complex proposals involve multiple Federal agencies along with State, local, and Tribal agencies. If another Federal, State, local, or Tribal agency has a major role in the proposed action and also has NEPA responsibilities or responsibilities under a similar NEPA-like law[17], that agency may be a "joint lead agency." A "joint lead agency" shares the lead agency's responsibility for management of the NEPA process, including public involvement and the preparation of documents. Other Federal, State, Tribal, or local government agencies may have a decision or special expertise regarding a proposed action, but less of a role than the lead agency. In that case, such a Federal, State, Tribal, or local government agency may be a "cooperating agency."

A "cooperating agency" is an agency that has jurisdiction by law or special expertise with respect to any environmental impact involved in a proposal (or a reasonable alternative). Thus, a "cooperating agency" typically will have some responsibilities for the analysis related to its jurisdiction or special expertise.

Once it has developed a proposed action, the agency will enter the initial analytical approach (Number 2 in Figure 1) to help it determine whether the agency will pursue the path of a Categorical Exclusion (CE), an Environmental Assessment (EA), or an Environmental Impact Statement (EIS).

---

[17] About a quarter of the states have such laws; for example, New York, Montana, Washington, and California all have such laws. New York City also has such a law. A list with references is available at *www.nepa.gov* by clicking on "State Information" or directly at *http://ceq.eh.doe.gov/nepa/states.html*.

Implementing the NEPA Process

Categorical Exclusions (CEs) (Number 3 in Figure 1)

A CE is a category of actions that the agency has determined does not individually or cumulatively have a significant effect on the quality of the human environment.[18] Examples include issuing administrative personnel procedures, making minor facility renovations (such as installing energy efficient lighting), and reconstruction of hiking trails on public lands. Agencies develop a list of CEs specific to their operations when they develop or revise their NEPA implementing procedures in accordance with CEQ's NEPA regulations.

A CE is based on an agency's experience with a particular kind of action and its environmental effects. The agency may have studied the action in previous EAs, found no significant impact on the environment based on the analyses, and validated the lack of significant impacts after the implementation. If this is the type of action that will be repeated over time, the agency may decide to amend their implementing regulations to include the action as a CE. In these cases, the draft agency procedures are published in the *Federal Register*, and a public comment period is required. Participation in these comment periods is an important way to be involved in the development of a particular CE.

---

[18] CEQ NEPA Regulations, 40 C.F.R. § 1508.4.

If a proposed action is included in the description provided for a listed CE established by the agency, the agency must check to make sure that no extraordinary circumstances exist that may cause the proposed action to have a significant effect in a particular situation. Extraordinary circumstances typically include such matters as effects to endangered species, protected cultural sites, and wetlands (Number 4 in Figure 1). If there are no extraordinary circumstances indicating that the effects of the action may be significant, then the agency can proceed with the action.

If the proposed action is not included in the description provided in the CE establised by the agency, or there are extraordinary circumstances, the agency must prepare an EA or an EIS, or develop a new proposal that may qualify for application of a CE. When the agency does not know or is uncertain whether significant impacts are expected, the agency should prepare an EA to determine if there are significant environmental effects.

Environmental Assessments (EA) (Number 5 in Figure 1)

The purpose of an EA is to determine the significance of the environmental effects and to look at alternative means to achieve the agency's objectives. The EA is intended to be a concise document that (1) briefly provides sufficient evidence and analysis for determining whether to prepare an EIS; (2) aids an agency's compliance with NEPA when no environmental impact statement is necessary; and (3) facilitates preparation of an Environmental Impact Statement when one is necessary.[19]

An EA should include brief discussions of:

- ❖ the need for the proposal,
- ❖ alternative courses of action for any proposal which involves unresolved conflicts concerning alternative uses of available resources,
- ❖ the environmental impacts of the proposed action and alternatives, and
- ❖ a listing of agencies and persons consulted.[20]

---

[19] CEQ NEPA Regulations, 40 C.F.R. § 1508.9.
[20] CEQ NEPA Regulations, 40 C.F.R. § 1508.9(b).

Because the EA serves to evaluate the significance of a proposal for agency actions, it should focus on the context and intensity of effects that may "significantly" affect the quality of the human environment.[21] Often the EA will identify ways in which the agency can revise the action to minimize environmental effects.

When preparing an EA, the agency has discretion as to the level of public involvement (Number 6 in Figure 1). The CEQ regulations state that the agency shall involve environmental agencies, applicants, and the public, to the extent practicable, in preparing EAs.[22] Sometimes agencies will choose to mirror the scoping and public comment periods that are found in the EIS process. In other situations, agencies make the EA and a draft FONSI available to interested members of the public.

Some agencies, such as the Army, require that interested parties be notified of the decision to prepare an EA, and the Army also makes the EA publicly available. Some agencies keep a notification list of parties interested in a particular kind of action or in all agency actions. Other agencies simply prepare the EA. Not all agencies systematically provide information about individual EAs, so it is important that you read the specific implementing procedures of the proposing agency or ask the local NEPA point of contact working on the project about the process and let the appropriate agency representative know if you are interested in being notified of all NEPA documents or NEPA processes related to a particular type of action.

The EA process concludes with either a Finding of No Significant Impact (FONSI) (Number 7 in Figure 1) or a determination to proceed to preparation of an EIS. A FONSI is a document that presents the reasons why the agency has concluded that there are no significant environmental impacts projected to occur upon implementation of the action.[23] The EA is either summarized in the FONSI or attached to it.

In two circumstances, the CEQ regulations require agencies to make the proposed FONSI available for public review for 30 days. Those situations are:

❖ if the type of proposed action hasn't been done before by the particular agency, or

---

[21] CEQ NEPA Regulations 40 C.F.R. § 1508.27.
[22] CEQ NEPA Regulations, 40 C.F.R. § 1501.4(e)(2).
[23] Government Printing Office Electronic Information Enhancement Act of 1993, 44 U.S.C. §§ 4101-4104.

❖ if the action is something that typically would require an EIS under the agency NEPA procedures.[24]

If this is the case, the FONSI is usually published in the *Federal Register*,[25] and the notice of availability of the FONSI will include information on how and where to provide your comments. If the requirement for a 30 day review is not triggered the FONSI often will not be published in the Federal Register. It may be posted on the agency's website, published in local newspapers or made available in some other manner. If you are interested in a particular action that is the subject of an EA, you should find out from the agency how it will make the FONSI available.

Environmental Impact Statements (EIS) (Number 8 in Figure 1)

A Federal agency must prepare an EIS if it is proposing a major federal action significantly affecting the quality of the human environment.[26] The regulatory requirements for an EIS are more detailed than the requirements for an EA or a categorical exclusion and are explained below.

Notice of Intent and Scoping (Numbers 9 and 10 in Figure 1)

The EIS process begins with publication of a Notice of Intent (NOI), stating the agency's intent to prepare an EIS for a particular proposal. (Number 9 in Figure 1). The NOI is published in the Federal Register, and provides some basic information on the proposed action in preparation for the scoping process (Number 10 in Figure 1).[27] The NOI provides a brief description of the proposed action and possible alternatives. It also describes the agency's proposed scoping process, including any meetings and how the public can get involved. The NOI will also contain an agency point of contact who can answer questions about the proposed action and the NEPA process.

The scoping process is the best time to identify issues, determine points of contact, establish project schedules, and provide recommendations to the agency. The overall goal is to define the scope of issues to be addressed in depth in the analyses that will be included in the EIS. Specifically, the scoping process will:

---

[24] 42 U.S.C. § 4332(C).

[25] Scoping is a NEPA term of art that describes one major public involvement aspect of the NEPA EIS process (CEQ NEPA Regulations, 40 C.F.R. § 1501.7).

[26] CEQ NEPA Regulations, 40 C.F.R. § 1501.7. More information on scoping can be found in CEQ's guidance on scoping at *www.nepa.gov*.

[27] Public hearings are run in a formal manner, with a recording or minutes taken of speakers' comments. Public meetings may be held in a variety of formats, and may be much more informal than hearings.

❖ Identify people or organizations who are interested in the proposed action;

❖ Identify the significant issues to be analyzed in the EIS;

❖ Identify and eliminate from detailed review those issues that will not be significant or those that have been adequately covered in prior environmental review;

❖ Determine the roles and responsibilities of lead and cooperating agencies;

❖ Identify any related EAs or EISs;

❖ Identify gaps in data and informational needs;

❖ Set time limits for the process and page limits for the EIS;

❖ Identify other environmental review and consultation requirements so they can be integrated with the EIS; and

❖ Indicate the relationship between the development of the environmental analysis and the agency's tentative decisionmaking schedule.[28]

As part of the process, agencies are required to identify and invite the participation of interested persons. The agency should choose whatever communications methods are best for effective involvement of communities, whether local, regional, or national, that are interested in the proposed action. Video conferencing, public meetings, conference calls, formal hearings, or informal workshops are among the legitimate ways to conduct scoping. It is in your interest to become involved as soon as the EIS process begins and to use the scoping opportunity to make thoughtful, rational presentations on impacts and alternatives. Some of the most constructive and beneficial interaction between the public and an agency occurs when citizens identify or develop reasonable alternatives that the agency can evaluate in the EIS.

---

[28] CEQ NEPA Regulations, 40 C.F.R. § 1501.7. More information on scoping can be found in CEQ's guidance on scoping at *www.nepa.gov* by clicking on "CEQ Guidance."

NEPA is About People and Places

Tent Rocks, Jemez Mountains.

Southern Regional NEPA Roundtable discussion on the NEPA Task Force report *Modernizing NEPA Implementation*

US District Courthouse, Sioux Falls, SD

From top left: Tent Rocks photo courtesy of www.lanl.gov; Courthouse, Sioux Falls, South Dakota, photo courtesy of General Services Administration, *http://rmrpbs.gsa.gov/internet/PBSWeb. nsf/0/ a704c21a7427f8d4872569b50079ac3d?OpenDocument*

Draft EIS (Number 11 in Figure 1)

The next major step in the EIS process that provides an opportunity for your input is when the agencies submit a draft EIS for public comment. The Environmental Protection Agency (EPA) publishes a Notice of Availability in the Federal Register informing you and other members of the public that the draft is available for comment (Number 12 in Figure 1). The EPA notices are also available at *http://www.epa.gov/compliance/nepa/eisdata.html*. Based on the communication plan established by the agency, websites, local papers, or other means of public notice may also be used. The comment period is at least 45 days long; however, it may be longer based on requirements spelled out in the agency specific NEPA procedures or at the agency's discretion. During this time, the agency may conduct public meetings or hearings as a way to solicit comments.[29] The agency will also request comments from other Federal, State, Tribal, and local agencies that may have jurisdiction or interest in the matter.

One key aspect of a draft EIS is the statement of the underlying purpose and need.[30] Agencies draft a "Purpose and Need" statement to describe what they are trying to achieve by proposing an action. The purpose and need statement explains to the reader why an agency action is necessary, and serves as the basis for identifying the reasonable alternatives that meet the purpose and need.

The identification and evaluation of alternative ways of meeting the purpose and need of the proposed action is the heart of the NEPA analysis. The lead agency or agencies must, "objectively evaluate all reasonable alternatives, and for alternatives which were eliminated from detailed study, briefly discuss the reasons for their having been eliminated."[31] Reasonable alternatives are those that substantially meet the agency's purpose and need. If the agency is considering an application for a permit or other federal approval, the agency must still consider all reasonable alternatives. Reasonable alternatives include those that are practical or feasible from the technical and economic standpoint and using common sense, rather than simply desirable from the standpoint of the applicant. Agencies are obligated to evaluate all reasonable alternatives or a range of reasonable alternatives in enough detail so that a reader can compare and contrast the environmental effects of the various alternatives.

---

[29] Public hearings are run in a formal manner, with a recording or minutes taken of speakers' comments. Public meetings may be held in a variety of formats, and may be much more informal than hearings.

[30] CEQ NEPA Regulations, 40 C.F.R. § 1502.13.

[31] CEQ NEPA Regulations, 40 C.F.R. § 1502.14.

Agencies must always describe and analyze a "no action alternative." The "no action" alternative is simply what would happen if the agency did not act upon the proposal for agency action. For example, in the case of an application to the U.S. Army Corps of Engineers for a permit to place fill in a particular area, the "no action" alternative is no permit. But in the case of a proposed new management plan for the National Park Service's management of a national park, the "no action" alternative is the continuation of the current management plan.

If an agency has a preferred alternative when it publishes a draft EIS, the draft must identify which alternative the agency prefers. All agencies must identify a preferred alternative in the final EIS, unless another law prohibits it from doing so.[32]

The agency must analyze the full range of direct, indirect, and cumulative effects of the preferred alternative, if any, and of the reasonable alternatives identified in the draft EIS. For purposes of NEPA, "effects" and "impacts" mean the same thing. They include ecological, aesthetic, historic, cultural, economic, social, or health impacts, whether adverse or beneficial.[33] It is important to note that human beings are part of the environment (indeed, that's why Congress used the phrase "human environment" in NEPA), so when an EIS is prepared and economic or social and natural or physical environmental effects are interrelated, the EIS should discuss all of these effects.[34]

CEQ NEPA Regulation Section 1508.8
[40 C.F.R. § 1508.8.]

"Effects" include:

(a) Direct effects, which are caused by the action and occur at the same time and place.

(b) Indirect effects, which are caused by the action and are later in time or farther removed in distance, but are still reasonably foreseeable. Indirect effects may include growth inducing effects and other effects related to induced changes in the pattern of land use, population density or growth rate, and related effects on air and water and other natural systems, including ecosystems.

Effects and impacts as used in these regulations are synonymous. Effects includes ecological (such as the effects on natural resources and on the components, structures, and functioning of affected ecosystems), aesthetic, historic, cultural, economic, social, or health, whether direct, indirect, or cumulative. Effects may also include those resulting from actions which may have both beneficial and detrimental effects, even if on balance the agency believes that the effect will be beneficial.

---

[32] CEQ NEPA Regulations, 40 C.F.R. § 1502.14(e).

[33] CEQ NEPA Regulations, 40 C.F.R. §§ 1508.7, 1508.8.

[34] CEQ NEPA Regulations, 40 C.F.R. § 1508.14.

In addition to the purpose and need, identification of reasonable alternatives, and the environmental effects of the alternatives, the draft EIS will contain a description of the environment that would be affected by the various alternatives.

The EIS will also have a list of who prepared the document and their qualifications,[35] a table of contents, and an index.[36] The agency may choose to include technical information in appendices that are either circulated with the draft or readily available for review.[37]

Final EIS (Number 13 in Figure 1)

When the public comment period is finished, the agency analyzes comments, conducts further analysis as necessary, and prepares the final EIS. In the final EIS, the agency must respond to the substantive comments received from other government agencies and from you and other members of the public.[38] The response can be in the form of changes in the final EIS, factual corrections, modifications to the analyses or the alternatives, new alternatives considered, or an explanation of why a comment does not require the agency's response.[39] Often the agency will meet with other agencies that may be affected by the proposed action in an effort to resolve an issue or mitigate project effects. A copy or a summary of your substantive comments and the response to them will be included in the final EIS.[40]

When it is ready, the agency will publish the final EIS and EPA will publish a Notice of Availability in the Federal Register. The Notice of Availability marks the start of a waiting period (Number 14 in Figure 1). A minimum of 30 days must pass before the agency can make a decision on their proposed action unless the agency couples the 30 days with a formal internal appeals process.[41] This provides time for the agency decisionmaker to consider the purpose and need, weigh the alternatives, balance their objectives, and make a decision.

There is an additional (but rarely used) procedure worth noting: pre-decision referrals to CEQ.[42] This referral process takes place when

---

[35] CEQ NEPA Regulations, 40 C.F.R. § 1502.17.
[36] CEQ NEPA Regulations, 40 C.F.R. § 1502.10.
[37] CEQ NEPA Regulations, 40 C.F.R. § 1502.18.
[38] CEQ NEPA Regulations, 40 C.F.R. § 1503.4.
[39] CEQ NEPA Regulations, 40 C.F.R. § 1503.4(a).
[40] CEQ NEPA Regulations, 40 C.F.R. § 1503.4(b).
[41] CEQ NEPA Regulations, 40 C.F.R. § 1506.10. If the end of the 30 day wait period is less than 90 days after the notice of availability of the Draft EIS, was published in the Federal Register, then the decision must await the expiration of the 90 days.
[42] CEQ NEPA Regulations, 40 C.F.R. part 1504.

EPA or another Federal agency determines that proceeding with the proposed action is environmentally unacceptable. If an agency reaches that conclusion, the agency can refer the issue to CEQ within 25 days after the Notice of Availability for the final EIS is issued. CEQ then works to resolve the issue with the agencies concerned. CEQ might also refer the agencies to the U.S. Institute for Environmental Conflict Resolution to try to address the matter before formal elevation.[43] There is no provision for citizens to formally refer an action to CEQ; however, CEQ typically provides an opportunity for public involvement in a referral.

Record of Decision (ROD) (Number 15 in Figure 1)

The ROD is the final step for agencies in the EIS process. The ROD is a document that states what the decision is; identifies the alternatives considered, including the environmentally preferred alternative; and discusses mitigation plans, including any enforcement and monitoring commitments.[44] In the ROD, the agency discusses all the factors, including any considerations of national policy, that were contemplated when it reached its decision on whether to, and if so how to, proceed with the proposed action. The ROD will also discuss if all practical means to avoid or minimize environmental harm have been adopted, and if not, why they were not.[45] The ROD is a publicly available document. Sometimes RODs are published in the Federal Register or on the agency's website, but if you are interested in receiving the ROD you should ask the agency's point of contact for the EIS how to obtain a copy of the ROD.

---

[43] The U.S. Institute reports disputes it is involved with to CEQ and requests concurrence from CEQ to engage in those disputes involving two or more federal agencies.

[44] CEQ NEPA Regulations, 40 C.F.R. § 1505.2.

[45] CEQ NEPA Regulations, 40 C.F.R. § 1505.2(c).

Environmental Management Systems (EMS)

Executive Order (EO 13423) and a subsequent memorandum issued from the Office of Management and Budget and CEQ direct all agencies to adopt an Environmental Management System (EMS). "An EMS is a systematic approach to identifying and managing an organization's environmental obligations and issues that can complement many aspects of the NEPA review process." (Boling, E.A. 2005. Environmental Management Systems and NEPA: A Framework for Productive Harmony. The Environmental Law Reporter. 35 ELR 10022. Environmental Law Institute). EMSs are typically used by organizations and agencies to set up the procedures that will help them comply with the specific requirements of environmental laws and regulations, such as air and water permits. EMSs can be particularly useful in NEPA in the context of post-decision monitoring and mitigation. Using the procedures provided by an EMS, agencies can better ensure they are proper implementation of mitigation measures and provide a mechanism for monitoring the actual effects of the mitigation. (CEQ, Aligning National Environmental Policy Act Processes with Environmental Management Systems — A Guide for NEPA and EMS Practitioners (April 2007) available at *www.nepa.gov* by clicking on "Aligning NEPA Processes with Environmental Mangement Systems.*"

Supplemental EIS (Asterisk in Figure 1)

Sometimes a Federal agency is obligated to prepare a supplement to an existing EIS. An agency must prepare a supplement to either a draft or final EIS if it makes substantial changes in the proposed action that are relevant to environmental concerns, or if there are significant new circumstances or information relevant to environmental concerns and bearing on the proposed action or its impacts. An agency may also prepare a supplemental EIS if it determines that doing so will further the purposes of NEPA.[46] A supplemental EIS is prepared in the same way as a draft or final EIS, except that scoping is not required. If a supplement is prepared following a draft EIS, the final EIS will address both the draft EIS and supplemental EIS.

---

[46] CEQ NEPA Regulations, 40 C.F.R. § 1502.9(c).

EPA's Review

EPA plays a critical role in other agencies' NEPA processes. EPA is required to review and provide comments on the adequacy of the analysis and the impact to the environment.[47] EPA uses a rating system that summarizes its recommendations to the lead agency (see Appendix C). If EPA determines that the action is environmentally unsatisfactory, it is required by law to refer the matter to CEQ.

The Office of Federal Activities in EPA is the official recipient of all EISs prepared by Federal agencies, and publishes the notices of availability in the Federal Register for all draft, final, and supplemental EISs. The publication of these notices start the official clock for public review and comment periods and wait periods.[48] In addition to the Federal Register, the notices and summaries of the EPA comments are available at *http://www.epa.gov/compliance/nepa/eisdata.html*.

When and How to Get Involved

It Depends on the Agency

To determine the specific steps in the process where public involvement will be the most effective, it is very important to review the agency's NEPA implementing procedures. As previously mentioned, NEPA processes differ among agencies. For example, the Federal Highway Administration provides a 30 day comment period (with or without a public meeting) on all EAs that they develop before a FONSI is issued while some other agencies have no required comment periods for EAs.[49]

In addition, new legislation can change the way NEPA is implemented in agencies. For example, after the passage of the "Safe, Accountable, Flexible, Efficient Transportation Equity Act", which is transportation legislation that Congress passed in August 2005, the Department of Transportation updated its NEPA processes to implement the new transportation legislation. The Federal Highway Administration and Federal Transit Administration have kept websites up to date and are tracking the evolving guidance at *http://www.environment.fhwa.dot.gov/strmlng/index.asp* by clicking on "SAFETEA-LU."

---

[47] Clean Air Act, 42 U.S.C. § 7609.

[48] CEQ NEPA Regulations, 40 C.F.R. § 1506.10.

[49] Federal Highway Administration NEPA Regulations, 23 C.F.R. § 771.119 (2005).

**Safe, Accountable, Flexible, Efficient
Transportation Equity Act:
A Legacy for Users
(SAFETEA-LU), Public Law 109-59**

Congress included some modifications to the regular NEPA process for proposed actions that require preparation of EISs in SAFETEA-LU. For example, SAFETEA-LU requires the lead agency to provide an opportunity as early as practicable during the environmental review process for the public to weigh in on both defining the purpose and need for a proposal and determining the range of alternatives to be considered. Congress provided for a process whereby some states could assume responsibilities for all environmental compliance, including NEPA. Congress also established a 180 day statute of limitations for lawsuits challenging agency approvals of projects.

If you are involved or anticipate becoming involved in the NEPA process for a proposed highway or federal mass transit proposal, you should become familiar with the specific requirements of SAFETEA-LU for the NEPA process. One good way to do this is check information on the Federal Highway Administration's website at *www.fhwa.dot.gov/safetealu*. By clicking on "Cross Reference" you will find both the requirements of the law and FHWA regulations and implementing guidance.

You should also be aware that in the context of highway planning, much work is done at a pre-NEPA stage through statewide, municipal, and rural planning processes. These processes often set the stage for the NEPA process and you should be aware of your opportunities to get involved at that earlier stage. You can learn more about these processes by going to the Federal Highway Administration's website listed above, or by obtaining a copy of "A Citizen's Guide to Transportation Decisionmaking", available at *www.fhwa.dot.gov/planning/citizen/index.htm* or by writing to the Federal Highway Administration at 1200 New Jersey Avenue, S.E., HEPP-20, Washington, D.C. 20590, Attention: Transportation Planning Capacity Building Team; or calling 202 366-0106. Another publication that may be of assistance is "The Metropolitan Transportation Planning Process: Key Issues. A Briefing Notebook for Transportation Decisionmakers, Officials, and Staff." That publication is being updated to reflect the changes in the SAFETEA-LU law, and should be available through the same website and addresses above.

Be Informed of Actions

Sometimes citizens are generally interested in actions taking place in a particular area (for example, in your community or in an ecosystem or a facility that affects you). If this is the case, you can inform the appropriate agency or agencies that you would like to be notified of any proposed action or any environmental impact analysis that might be prepared in that area. In addition, many agencies now have websites where they post notices for actions they are proposing.

Active Involvement

Being active in the NEPA process requires you to dedicate your resources to the effort. Environmental impact analyses can be technical and lengthy. Active involvement in the NEPA process requires a commitment of time and a willingness to share information with the decisionmaking agency and other citizens. You may participate as an individual, get involved by working with other interested individuals or organizations, or by working through your local, Tribal, or State government. For example, if an agency is taking an action for which your local, State or Tribal government has special expertise or approval authority, the appropriate State, local or Tribal agency can become a "cooperating agency" with the Federal agency.[50] This formal status does not increase their role in decisionmaking, but it does allow the governments to use their knowledge and authorities to help shape the federal decisionmaking.

Another way to participate is to check with local experts such as biologists or economists at a university to assist with your review of the NEPA analyses and documents. You can also form study groups to review environmental impact analyses and enlist experts to review your comments on the documents. There are many examples, such as the one in the following box, of situations where citizen groups have worked with agencies to develop an alternative to a proposal where the agency adopted that alternative.

---

[50] CEQ NEPA Regulations, 40 C.F.R. §§ 1501.6, 1508.5.

Forest Service Herbicide Use in the Pacific Northwest

In many cases, cooperation isn't the first experience that communities and agencies share with one another. In the case of aerial herbicide spraying by the Forest Service in the 1980's across Washington and Oregon, litigation gave way to collaboration that yielded a better decision for all parties.

At issue was the use of 2,4-D, a herbicide comprising half of the well known Agent Orange, which was being sprayed on large tracts of clear-cut forest in an effort to suppress competition with the replanted conifers from all other plants, including native trees and grasses. In 1984, as a result of a citizen lawsuit, a federal judge ordered the Forest Service to stop herbicide use until the agency addressed the problems associated with its use. The Forest Service decided to draft a new EIS for vegetation management and thereby opened the door for public involvement in their decision.

A coalition of tree planters, scientists, rural residents, and herbicide reform activists volunteered to work with the Forest Service to develop an alternative that didn't rely on herbicides for vegetation management. The group identified several simple alternatives such as planting two-year old trees rather than planting seedlings, because the trees are better able to deal with encroachment. Likewise, letting native red alders grow will actually benefit new conifer growth because the alders fix nitrogen in the soils. Much to the coalition's surprise the forest supervisor selected most of the "least-herbicide" approaches for implementation.

Through NEPA, citizens were able to educate and assist the decision-makers in developing their alternatives. Central to their approach was bringing to the table alternatives that met their goals of reducing herbicide use and the goals of the decision-maker to effectively manage vegetation.

Information taken from "Standing Up for This World" by Mary O'Brien in September/October 2004 issue of *Orion*, pages 56-64.

Your involvement in the NEPA process does not have to be confined to commenting on the analysis. If the agency adopts monitoring and mitigation in the ROD, upon request, it must make available to the public the results of relevant monitoring.[51] It must also, upon request,

---

[51] CEQ NEPA Regulations, 40 C.F.R. §1505.3(d).

inform cooperating or commenting agencies on progress in carrying out mitigation measures which they have proposed and which were adopted by the agency making the decision.[52] Community groups can also be involved in monitoring.[53]

In summary, there are several opportunities to get involved in the NEPA process:

- ❖ when the agency prepares its NEPA procedures,

- ❖ prior to and during preparation of a NEPA analysis,

- ❖ when a NEPA document is published for public review and comment, and

- ❖ when monitoring the implementation of the proposed action and the effectiveness of any associated mitigation.

Other Processes that Require Public Involvement

When a proposed action is part of a permitting process there may also be opportunities to comment provided in the statute or regulations for that permitting process in addition to the NEPA public involvement opportunities discussed above. For example, public involvement is required by most Federal agency land use planning regulations. While this guide does not explore all of those additional possibilities for comment, the NEPA team working on a particular proposal will be familiar with the various comment periods and will be able to inform you of those opportunities. Note that the permitting and NEPA processes should be integrated or run concurrently in order to have an effective and efficient decisionmaking process.

---

[52] CEQ NEPA Regulations, 40 C.F.R. §1505.3(c).

[53] See *www.malpaiborderlandsgroup.org/science.asp* for discussion of work undertaken by the Science Advisory Committee of the Malpai Borderlands Group in southeastern Arizona and southwestern New Mexico.

Public Comment Periods

Agencies are required to make efforts to provide meaningful public involvement in their NEPA processes.[54] Citizens involved in the process should ensure that they know how agencies will inform the public that an action is proposed and the NEPA process is beginning (via Federal Register, newspapers, direct mailing, etc.); that certain documents are available; and that preliminary determinations have been made on the possible environmental effects of the proposal (e.g., what level of analysis the agency will initially undertake).

Agencies solicit different levels of involvement when they prepare an EA versus an EIS. In preparing an EIS, agencies are likely to have public meetings and are required to have a 45 day comment period after the draft EIS is made available. In the case of an agency preparing an EA, the CEQ regulations require the agency to involve the public to the extent practicable, but each agency has its own guidelines about how to involve the public for EAs. In any case, citizens are entitled to receive "environmental documents", such as EAs, involved in the NEPA process.[55]

In terms of a specific agency, required public comment periods associated with an EA or an EIS can be found in its NEPA implementing procedures. In some cases, the draft EIS that an agency prepares may be extremely long. In such cases, an agency may grant, requests to extend the comment period to ensure enough time for the public and other agencies to review and comment.

Citizens who want to raise issues with the agency should do so at the earliest possible stage in the process. Agencies are much more likely to evaluate a new alternative or address a concern if it is raised in a timely manner. And the Supreme Court has held in two NEPA cases that if a person or organization expects courts to address an issue, such as evaluating a particular alternative, the issue must have been raised to the agency at a point in the administrative process when it can be meaningfully considered unless the issue involves a flaw in the agency's analysis that is so obvious that there is no need for a commentator to point it out specifically.

---

[54] CEQ NEPA Regulations, 40 C.F.R. §§ 1501.4(b), 1506.6(b).
[55] CEQ NEPA Regulations, 40 C.F.R. §§ 1506.6, 1508.10.

How to Comment

Comments may be the most important contribution from citizens. Accordingly, comments should be clear, concise, and relevant to the analysis of the proposed action. Take the time to organize thoughts and edit the document submitted.[56] As a general rule, the tone of the comments should be polite and respectful. Those reviewing comments are public servants tasked with a job, and they deserve the same respect and professional treatment that you and other citizens expect in return. Comments that are solution oriented and provide specific examples will be more effective than those that simply oppose the proposed project. Comments that contribute to developing alternatives that address the purpose and need for the action are also effective. They are particularly helpful early in the NEPA process and should be made, if at all possible, during scoping, to ensure that reasonable alternatives can be analyzed and considered early in the process.

In drafting comments, try to focus on the purpose and need of the proposed action, the proposed alternatives, the assessment of the environmental impacts of those alternatives, and the proposed mitigation. It also helps to be aware of what other types of issues the decisionmaker is considering in relationship to the proposed action.

Commenting is not a form of "voting" on an alternative. The number of negative comments an agency receives does not prevent an action from moving forward. Numerous comments that repeat the same basic message of support or opposition will typically be responded to collectively. In addition, general comments that state an action will have "significant environmental effects" will not help an agency make a better decision unless the relevant causes and environmental effects are explained.

Finally, remember that decisionmakers also receive other information and data such as operational and technical information related to implementing an action that they will have to consider when making a final decision.

---

[56] There are many reference books for how to research issues, review documents, and write comments. One in particular is "The Art of Commenting" by Elizabeth Mullin from the Environmental Law Institute (Mullin, Elizabeth D. 2000. t The Art of Commenting: How to Influence Environmental Decisionmaking with Effective Comments, Environmental Law Institute. Washington, DC). Another useful reference for those involved in commenting on transportation projects is the American Association of State Highway and Transportation Official's (AASHTO) Practitioner's Handbook 05-Utilizing Community Advisory Committees for NEPA Studies, December, 2006, available at *http://environment.transportation.org* or available through AASHTO's Center for Environmental Excellence by calling (202) 624-3635.

What If Involvement Isn't Going Well?

For the purposes of this discussion, "not going well" means that you or your organization believes that the lead agency isn't giving the public sufficient opportunity to get involved or isn't using that involvement effectively. Perhaps you think that the agency should hold a public meeting, and it refuses to do so. Or you or your community or group has developed an alternative that you think meets the purpose and need of the proposed action and reflects the policies set forth in NEPA, but the agency says it won't analyze it in the NEPA document. Maybe you want an extension of the comment period because the document is very lengthy, and you simply need more time to review it. Or maybe you feel that communications between your organization and the lead agency have, for some reason, not been constructive.

The most appropriate steps to take if you find yourself in these kinds of situations always depend, of course, on the particular people, timing and proposal at hand. Nonetheless, here are some possible factors and courses of action to consider.

Don't Wait Too Long

First, don't wait too long to raise your concerns; raise them as soon as practicable. If you just sit back and hope that things will get "better" or that your comments will have greater effect later, you may hear that "you should have raised this sooner." At times, waiting can be detrimental to you as well as to the rest of the public and the agency involved. For example, if you feel strongly that a particular alternative should be addressed and do not raise it during the scoping process, then it will not get the benefit of comparative analysis with the other alternatives. In addition, it could result in a more expensive and lengthy process (costing taxpayers, including yourself, more) if your delayed suggestion results in the agency deciding to issue a supplemental EIS analyzing that alternative. Or if you, or your organization, later go to court to argue that a certain alternative should have been analyzed in the NEPA document, the judge may find that the court won't consider that information because you should have raised your concern earlier during the NEPA process.

Contact the Agency

Your first line of recourse should be with the individual that the agency has identified as being in charge of this particular process.

See if you can sit down with him or her to discuss your concern(s). You may be pleasantly surprised at the response.

Other Assistance

If, for some reason, you believe that the process ahead may be particularly contentious or challenging, given a past history of community conflict or deeply divided interests, consider raising with the lead agency the possibility of designing a collaborative process with outside assistance.

One source of such assistance is the U.S. Institute for Environmental Conflict Resolution. Located in Tucson, Arizona, as part of the Morris K. Udall Foundation, the Institute is a Federal entity that offers neutral environmental conflict resolution design, facilitation, education, training, and mediation. Anyone, whether in or out of government, can call the Institute and ask to speak to a professional staff person to discuss the potential for the Institute's involvement in a proposed federal action. You might want to look at its website at www.ecr.gov or contact the Institute to get a better sense of who they are and what they do.[57] There may also be an environmental conflict resolution office in your state that can provide assistance, and there are also many other individuals and organizations in the private sector that provide various types of conflict resolution services. The U.S. Institute also maintains a publicly accessible roster of environmental mediators and facilitators (available at *www.ecr.gov* by clicking on "Resources").

NEPA's Requirements

Perhaps your concern involves understanding a legal requirement. There are, of course, many ways to obtain the advice of lawyers knowledgeable about the NEPA process: the lead agency, private attorneys, and public interest attorneys. Build your own understanding by reading information on the NEPA net website at *http://www.NEPA.gov*. You may also call the General Counsel's office or the Associate Director for NEPA Oversight at the Council on Environmental Quality for assistance in interpreting NEPA's legal requirements or for advice and assistance if you have tried to work with the lead agency but feel those efforts have been unsuccessful (see Appendix D for contact information).

---

[57] The Institute can be contacted via mailing address: U.S. Institute for Environmental Conflict Resolution, 130 S. Scott Ave. Tucson, AZ 85701; phone: (520) 901-8501; or electronic mail: usiecr@ecr.gov. You might also be interested in reviewing the April 2005 report of the National Environmental Conflict Resolution Advisory Committee that discusses the linkages between NEPA's policies and environmental conflict resolution and is available at *http://www.ecr.gov* by clicking on "Resources" and "NEPA and ECR".

Remedies Available

Finally, of course, there are both administrative and judicial remedies available. A few Federal agencies, such as the Bureau of Land Management and the Forest Service, have an administrative appeals process. Each process is specific to that agency. If an appeal is available, you may find it beneficial to invoke it to try to resolve your concerns with the agency's decisions without the need for a legal challenge. Moreover, a statute or agency regulation may require you to exhaust such an appeal procedure before seeking judicial review. Citizens who believe that a Federal agency's actions violate NEPA may seek judicial review (after any required administrative appeals) in Federal court under the Administration Procedures Act. If you are represented by a lawyer, you should consult with him or her about appropriate options and about communicating with the Federal agencies.

Final Thoughts

This guide was developed to explain the National Environmental Policy Act (NEPA), how it is implemented, and how people outside the Federal government — individual citizens, private sector applicants, members of organized groups, or representatives of Tribal, State, or local government agencies — can better participate in the assessment of environmental impacts conducted by Federal agencies. To learn more about CEQ and NEPA, visit our web sites at *http://www.whitehouse.gov/ceq* and *http://www.nepa.gov* or contact the CEQ Associate Director for NEPA Oversight at (202) 395-5750. Your thoughts and comments on improving this Guide for future editions are always welcome and can be addressed to:

CEQ NEPA Citizens Guide
722 Jackson Place, NW
Washington, DC 20503

Appendix A

NEPAnet and How to Use It

NEPAnet
http://www.NEPA.gov

NEPAnet is the Council on Environmental Quality's NEPA website which is supported by the Department of Energy. It contains a wealth of information related to NEPA as it has developed over the years in agencies and through the courts. Guidance as well as studies and reports from CEQ can be accessed from the site; and information on NEPA training can also be found.

Under the "National Environmental Policy Act (NEPA)" section there are several useful links including:

❖ The NEPA Statute

❖ Executive Orders

❖ CEQ Regulations for Implementing NEPA

❖ Individual Federal Agency Procedures for Implementing NEPA*

❖ CEQ Guidance; topics include:

— Environmental Conflict Resolution

— Emergency Actions

— Cumulative Effects Analysis

— Cooperating Agencies

* The agency implementing procedures can be accessed here and are mentioned throughout the Citizen's Guide as an important part of the process.

- — Purpose and Need
- — Forest Health Projects
- — Environmental Justice
- — Transboundary Impacts
- — Pollution Prevention
- — Scoping
- — Forty Most Asked Questions Concerning CEQ's NEPA Regulations
- — Wetlands
- — Prime Agricultural Land
- — Wild and Scenic Rivers
- ❖ Federal Agency NEPA Web Sites
- ❖ Federal NEPA Contacts
- ❖ State Information
- ❖ Tribal Information

The other sections provide information about:

- ❖ CEQ NEPA Studies
- ❖ CEQ NEPA Reports
- ❖ Environmental Impact Statements
- ❖ Environmental Impact Analysis
- ❖ Environmental Impact Assessment Professional Organizations
- ❖ International Environmental Impact Assessments
- ❖ NEPA Litigation
- ❖ NEPA Case law
- ❖ NEPA Training Information

Appendix B

The Federal Register and How to Use It

http://www.gpoaccess.gov/fr/index.html

The Federal Register is the official daily publication for rules, proposed rules, and notices of Federal agencies and organizations, as well as executive orders and other presidential documents. It is updated daily by 6 a.m. and is published Monday through Friday, except Federal holidays.

This is where you'll find notices from Federal agencies regarding their NEPA actions. Information on the availability of documents, schedule of meetings, and notices of intent to prepare EISs are also published in the Federal Register. In addition, EPA publishes a list of EISs that they have received from agencies each week, and a summary of ratings on EISs that they have reviewed.

The easiest way to pull up notices is to have as much information as possible. Key words such as the name of the agency, location of the action, date or date ranges of the publication are all helpful in the search.

Appendix C

EPA's EIS Rating System

EPA's Environmental Impact Statement Rating System Criteria
http://www.epa.gov/compliance/nepa/comments/ratings.html

This website includes information about EISs that have been filed with EPA, EISs that are available for public comment, and information about EPA's review and rating of individual EISs.

EPA has developed a set of criteria for rating draft EISs. The rating system provides a basis upon which EPA makes recommendations to the lead agency for improving the draft EIS.

❖ Rating the Environmental Impact of the Action

❖ Rating the Adequacy of the Draft Environmental Impact Statement (EIS)

Rating The Environmental Impact of The Action

❖ **LO (Lack of Objections):** The review has not identified any potential environmental impacts requiring substantive changes to the preferred alternative. The review may have disclosed opportunities for application of mitigation measures that could be accomplished with no more than minor changes to the proposed action.

❖ **EC (Environmental Concerns):** The review has identified environmental impacts that should be avoided in order to fully protect the environment. Corrective measures may require changes to the preferred alternative or application of mitigation measures that can reduce the environmental impact.

❖ **EO (Environmental Objections):** The review has identified significant environmental impacts that should be avoided in order to adequately protect the environment. Corrective measures may require substantial changes to the preferred alternative or consideration of some other project alternative (including the no action alternative or a new alternative). The basis for environmental Objections can include situations:

1. Where an action might violate or be inconsistent with achievement or maintenance of a national environmental standard;

2. Where the Federal agency violates its own substantive environmental requirements that relate to EPA's areas of jurisdiction or expertise;

3. Where there is a violation of an EPA policy declaration;

4. Where there are no applicable standards or where applicable standards will not be violated but there is potential for significant environmental degradation that could be corrected by project modification or other feasible alternatives; or

5. Where proceeding with the proposed action would set a precedent for future actions that collectively could result in significant environmental impacts.

❖ **EU (Environmentally Unsatisfactory):** The review has identified adverse environmental impacts that are of sufficient magnitude that EPA believes the proposed action must not proceed as proposed. The basis for an environmentally unsatisfactory determination consists of identification of environmentally objectionable impacts as defined above and one or more of the following conditions:

1. The potential violation of or inconsistency with a national environmental standard is substantive and/or will occur on a long-term basis;

2. There are no applicable standards but the severity, duration, or geographical scope of the impacts associated with the proposed action warrant special attention; or

3. The potential environmental impacts resulting from the proposed action are of national importance because of the threat to national environmental resources or to environmental policies.

Rating The Adequacy of The Draft Environmental Impact Statement (EIS)

❖ **1 (Adequate):** The draft EIS adequately sets forth the environmental impact(s) of the preferred alternative and those of the alternatives reasonably available to the project or action. No further analysis or data collection is necessary, but the reviewer may suggest the addition of clarifying language or information.

❖ **2 (Insufficient Information):** The draft EIS does not contain sufficient information to fully assess environmental impacts that should be avoided in order to fully protect the environment, or the reviewer has identified new reasonably available alternatives that are within the spectrum of alternatives analyzed in the draft EIS, which could reduce the environmental impacts of the proposal. The identified additional information, data, analyses, or discussion should be included in the final EIS.

❖ **3 (Inadequate):** The draft EIS does not adequately assess the potentially significant environmental impacts of the proposal, or the reviewer has identified new, reasonably available, alternatives that are outside of the spectrum of alternatives analyzed in the draft EIS, which should be analyzed in order to reduce the potentially significant environmental impacts. The identified additional information, data, analyses, or discussions are of such a magnitude that they should have full public review at a draft stage. This rating indicates EPA's belief that the draft EIS does not meet the purposes of NEPA and/or the Section 309 review, and thus should be formally revised and made available for public comment in a supplemental or revised draft EIS.

Appendix D

Agency NEPA Contacts

http://www.NEPA.gov
http://ceq.eh.doe.gov/nepa/contacts.cfm

The list of Federal NEPA Contacts is maintained on NEPAnet (*http://www.NEPA.gov*) under the heading "National Environmental Policy Act (NEPA)" and is periodically updated.

The complete list is available via the link entitled "Federal NEPA Contacts" or available directly at *http://ceq.eh.doe.gov/nepa/contacts.cfm*. If you do not have computer access, call CEQ at (202) 395-5750 for assistance.

The CEQ NEPA Contacts are:

Council on Environmental Quality
722 Jackson Place, NW
Washington, DC 20503
Phone: 202-395-5750
Fax: 202-456-6546

Mr. Horst Greczmiel, Associate Director for NEPA Oversight
Ms. Dinah Bear, General Counsel
Mr. Edward (Ted) Boling, Deputy General Counsel

Appendix E

**Some Useful Definitions from the
Council on Environmental Quality
NEPA Implementing Regulations**

Excerpts from 40 CFR part 1508
http://ceq.eh.doe.gov/nepa/regs/ceq/toc_ceq.htm

Section 1508.4 Categorical exclusion.

"Categorical exclusion" means a category of actions which do not individually or cumulatively have a significant effect on the human environment and which have been found to have no such effect in procedures adopted by a Federal agency in implementation of these regulations (Sec. 1507.3) and for which, therefore, neither an environmental assessment nor an environmental impact statement is required. An agency may decide in its procedures or otherwise, to prepare environmental assessments for the reasons stated in Sec. 1508.9 even though it is not required to do so. Any procedures under this section shall provide for extraordinary circumstances in which a normally excluded action may have a significant environmental effect.

Section 1508.5 Cooperating agency.

"Cooperating agency" means any Federal agency other than a lead agency which has jurisdiction by law or special expertise with respect to any environmental impact involved in a proposal (or a reasonable alternative) for legislation or other major Federal action significantly affecting the quality of the human environment. The selection and responsibilities of a cooperating agency are described in Sec. 1501.6. A State or local agency of similar qualifications or, when the effects are on a reservation, an Indian Tribe, may by agreement with the lead agency become a cooperating agency.

Section 1508.7 Cumulative impact.

"Cumulative impact" is the impact on the environment which results from the incremental impact of the action when added to other past, present, and reasonably foreseeable future actions regardless of what agency (Federal or non-federal) or person undertakes such other actions. Cumulative impacts can result from individually minor but collectively significant actions taking place over a period of time.

Section 1508.8 Effects.

"Effects" include:

> (a) Direct effects, which are caused by the action and occur at the same time and place.

> (b) Indirect effects, which are caused by the action and are later in time or farther removed in distance, but are still reasonably foreseeable. Indirect effects may include growth inducing effects and other effects related to induced changes in the pattern of land use, population density or growth rate, and related effects on air and water and other natural systems, including ecosystems.

Effects and impacts as used in these regulations are synonymous. Effects includes ecological (such as the effects on natural resources and on the components, structures, and functioning of affected ecosystems), aesthetic, historic, cultural, economic, social, or health, whether direct, indirect, or cumulative. Effects may also include those resulting from actions which may have both beneficial and detrimental effects, even if on balance the agency believes that the effect will be beneficial.

Section 1508.9 Environmental assessment.

"Environmental assessment":

> (a) Means a concise public document for which a Federal agency is responsible that serves to:

> 1. Briefly provide sufficient evidence and analysis for determining whether to prepare an environmental impact statement or a finding of no significant impact.

> 2. Aid an agency's compliance with the Act when no environmental impact statement is necessary.

> 3. Facilitate preparation of a statement when one is necessary.

(b) Shall include brief discussions of the need for the proposal, of alternatives as required by section 102(2)(E), of the environmental impacts of the proposed action and alternatives, and a listing of agencies and persons consulted.

Section 1508.11 Environmental impact statement.

"Environmental impact statement" means a detailed written statement as required by section 102(2)(C) of the Act.

Section 1508.12 Federal agency.

"Federal agency" means all agencies of the Federal Government. It does not mean the Congress, the Judiciary, or the President, including the performance of staff functions for the President in his Executive Office. It also includes for purposes of these regulations States and units of general local government and Indian Tribes assuming NEPA responsibilities under section 104(h) of the Housing and Community Development Act of 1974.

Section 1508.13 Finding of no significant impact.

"Finding of no significant impact" means a document by a Federal agency briefly presenting the reasons why an action, not otherwise excluded (Sec. 1508.4), will not have a significant effect on the human environment and for which an environmental impact statement therefore will not be prepared. It shall include the environmental assessment or a summary of it and shall note any other environmental documents related to it (Sec. 1501.7(a)(5)). If the assessment is included, the finding need not repeat any of the discussion in the assessment but may incorporate it by reference.

Section 1508.14 Human environment.

"Human environment" shall be interpreted comprehensively to include the natural and physical environment and the relationship of people with that environment. (See the definition of "effects" (Sec. 1508.8).) This means that economic or social effects are not intended by themselves to require preparation of an environmental impact statement. When an environmental impact statement is prepared and economic or social and natural or physical environmental effects are interrelated, then the environmental impact statement will discuss all of these effects on the human environment.

Section 1508.16 Lead agency.

"Lead agency" means the agency or agencies preparing or having taken primary responsibility for preparing the environmental impact statement.

Section 1508.18 Major federal action.

"Major federal action" includes actions with effects that may be major and which are potentially subject to federal control and responsibility. Major reinforces but does not have a meaning independent of significantly (Sec. 1508.27). Actions include the circumstance where the responsible officials fail to act and that failure to act is reviewable by courts or administrative tribunals under the Administrative Procedure Act or other applicable law as agency action.

> (a) Actions include new and continuing activities, including projects and programs entirely or partly financed, assisted, conducted, regulated, or approved by Federal agencies; new or revised agency rules, regulations, plans, policies, or procedures; and legislative proposals (Secs. 1506.8, 1508.17). Actions do not include funding assistance solely in the form of general revenue sharing funds, distributed under the State and Local Fiscal Assistance Act of 1972, 31 U.S.C. 1221 et seq., with no Federal agency control over the subsequent use of such funds. Actions do not include bringing judicial or administrative civil or criminal enforcement actions.
>
> (b) Federal actions tend to fall within one of the following categories:
>
> 1. Adoption of official policy, such as rules, regulations, and interpretations adopted pursuant to the Administrative Procedure Act, 5 U.S.C. 551 et seq.; treaties and international conventions or agreements; formal documents establishing an agency's policies which will result in or substantially alter agency programs.
>
> 2. Adoption of formal plans, such as official documents prepared or approved by Federal agencies which guide or prescribe alternative uses of federal resources, upon which future agency actions will be based.

3. Adoption of programs, such as a group of concerted actions to implement a specific policy or plan; systematic and connected agency decisions allocating agency resources to implement a specific statutory program or executive directive.

4. Approval of specific projects, such as construction or management activities located in a defined geographic area. Projects include actions approved by permit or other regulatory decision as well as federal and federally assisted activities.

Section 1508.20 Mitigation.

"Mitigation" includes:

(a) Avoiding the impact altogether by not taking a certain action or parts of an action.

(b) Minimizing impacts by limiting the degree or magnitude of the action and its implementation.

(c) Rectifying the impact by repairing, rehabilitating, or restoring the affected environment.

(d) Reducing or eliminating the impact over time by preservation and maintenance operations during the life of the action.

(e) Compensating for the impact by replacing or providing substitute resources or environments.

Section 1508.22 Notice of intent.

"Notice of intent" means a notice that an environmental impact statement will be prepared and considered. The notice shall briefly:

(a) Describe the proposed action and possible alternatives.

(b) Describe the agency's proposed scoping process including whether, when, and where any scoping meeting will be held.

(c) State the name and address of a person within the agency who can answer questions about the proposed action and the environmental impact statement.

Section 1508.23 Proposal.

"Proposal" exists at that stage in the development of an action when an agency subject to the Act has a goal and is actively preparing to make a decision on one or more alternative means of accomplishing that goal and the effects can be meaningfully evaluated. Preparation of an environmental impact statement on a proposal should be timed (Sec. 1502.5) so that the final statement may be completed in time for the statement to be included in any recommendation or report on the proposal. A proposal may exist in fact as well as by agency declaration that one exists.

Section 1508.25 Scope.

"Scope" consists of the range of actions, alternatives, and impacts to be considered in an environmental impact statement. The scope of an individual statement may depend on its relationships to other statements (Secs.1502.20 and 1508.28). To determine the scope of environmental impact statements, agencies shall consider 3 types of actions, 3 types of alternatives, and 3 types of impacts. They include:

(a) Actions (other than unconnected single actions) which may be:

(1) Connected actions, which means that they are closely related and therefore should be discussed in the same impact statement. Actions are connected if they:

(i) Automatically trigger other actions which may require environmental impact statements.

(ii) Cannot or will not proceed unless other actions are taken previously or simultaneously.

(iii) Are interdependent parts of a larger action and depend on the larger action for their justification.

(2) Cumulative actions, which when viewed with other proposed actions have cumulatively significant impacts and should therefore be discussed in the same impact statement.

(3) Similar actions, which when viewed with other reasonably foreseeable or proposed agency actions, have similarities that provide a basis for evaluating their environmental consequencies together, such as common timing or geography. An agency may

wish to analyze these actions in the same impact statement. It should do so when the best way to assess adequately the combined impacts of similar actions or reasonable alternatives to such actions is to treat them in a single impact statement.

(b) Alternatives, which include:

(1) No action alternative.

(2) Other reasonable courses of actions.

(3) Mitigation measures (not in the proposed action).

(c) Impacts, which may be: (1) Direct; (2) indirect; (3) cumulative.

Section 1508.27 Significantly.

"Significantly" as used in NEPA requires considerations of both context and intensity:

(a) Context. This means that the significance of an action must be analyzed in several contexts such as society as a whole (human, national), the affected region, the affected interests, and the locality. Significance varies with the setting of the proposed action. For instance, in the case of a site-specific action, significance would usually depend upon the effects in the locale rather than in the world as a whole. Both short- and long-term effects are relevant.

(b) Intensity. This refers to the severity of impact. Responsible officials must bear in mind that more than one agency may make decisions about partial aspects of a major action. The following should be considered in evaluating intensity:

(1) Impacts that may be both beneficial and adverse. A significant effect may exist even if the Federal agency believes that on balance the effect will be beneficial.

(2) The degree to which the proposed action affects public health or safety.

(3) Unique characteristics of the geographic area such as proximity to historic or cultural resources, park

lands, prime farmlands, wetlands, wild and scenic rivers, or ecologically critical areas.

(4) The degree to which the effects on the quality of the human environment are likely to be highly controversial.

(5) The degree to which the possible effects on the human environment are highly uncertain or involve unique or unknown risks.

(6) The degree to which the action may establish a precedent for future actions with significant effects or represents a decision in principle about a future consideration.

(7) Whether the action is related to other actions with individually insignificant but cumulatively significant impacts. Significance exists if it is reasonable to anticipate a cumulatively significant impact on the environment. Significance cannot be avoided by terming an action temporary or by breaking it down into small component parts.

(8) The degree to which the action may adversely affect districts, sites, highways, structures, or objects listed in or eligible for listing in the National Register of Historic Places or may cause loss or destruction of significant scientific, cultural, or historical resources.

(9) The degree to which the action may adversely affect an endangered or threatened species or its habitat that has been determined to be critical under the Endangered Species Act of 1973.

(10) Whether the action threatens a violation of Federal, State, or local law or requirements imposed for the protection of the environment.

Section 1508.28 Tiering.

"Tiering" refers to the coverage of general matters in broader environmental impact statements (such as national program or policy statements) with subsequent narrower statements or environmental analyses (such as regional or basinwide program statements or ultimately site-specific statements) incorporating by reference the general discussions and concentrating solely on the issues specific to the statement subsequently prepared. Tiering is appropriate when the sequence of statements or analyses is:

(a) From a program, plan, or policy environmental impact statement to a program, plan, or policy statement or analysis of lesser scope or to a site-specific statement or analysis.

(b) From an environmental impact statement on a specific action at an early stage (such as need and site selection) to a supplement (which is preferred) or a subsequent statement or analysis at a later stage (such as environmental mitigation). Tiering in such cases is appropriate when it helps the lead agency to focus on the issues which are ripe for decision and exclude from consideration issues already decided or not yet ripe.